Wyoming:

The Next Question to Ask
(to Answer)

poems by

Tyler Truman Julian

Finishing Line Press
Georgetown, Kentucky

Wyoming:

The Next Question to Ask
(to Answer)

ACKNOWLEDGMENTS

There are many people I need to thank for helping make this book a reality:

Sarah Suzor, thank you, darling, for pushing me beyond what I thought I could do and being my therapist every week as we picked apart this book. I wouldn't have wanted it any other way. "Meet me at the Mint" because I owe you a drink.

Breanna Farley, thank you for being willing to enter this new life with me. I am so happy I can do it with you at my side.

My family: Thank you for always being my first reader, Mom. And thank you, Dad, Katelynn, and Emily for believing in this. I owe a special thanks to Garrett whose words became part of this book as we sat around a fire drinking cheap whiskey, and thank you to the rest who I love deeply. I hope you find this book meaningful.

Nina Welch, thank you for taking me out to dance across Paris, red wine in hand. This book is for you and our friendship.

Erin Abraham, thank you for helping me piece together the very first draft of this book and for challenging me in beautiful and powerful ways.

Thank you Chelsea Dingman, Travis Cebula, and Craig Johnson for reading and supporting this book with your words, and a very special thanks goes to Finishing Line Press for taking a chance on this strange little book.

Publisher: Leah Maines
Editor: Christen Kincaid
Cover Art: Tyler Truman Julian
Author Photo: Kelli Campbell, Kelli Campbell Photography
Cover Design: Leah Huete

Printed in the USA on acid-free paper.
Order online: www.finishinglinepress.com
also available on amazon.com

Author inquiries and mail orders:
Finishing Line Press
P. O. Box 1626
Georgetown, Kentucky 40324
U. S. A.

Table of Contents

To Be Read Almost In Real Time

For Nina Welch,
who is younger still than my seventy year old soul…

West is just west
and it never runs out.

—Sarah Suzor, *The Principle Agent*

Wyoming
has a little more
than half a million people;
it's around 563,626,
it's just easier to say half a million.

All of us
are spread out
across 97,914 square miles,
about 5 people per mile,
but your closest neighbor might really be 15 miles away.

One might ask, naturally:
Who does leave this place and why?

A Figment of 'Magination

Wyoming

Have you seen the pines turn blue
as the light changes to night,
wondering if pine or spruce or fir
smell of vanilla?
Or the flowers wilt in the artificial light,
forcing the stars to burn a little brighter
just for you?
Like cyclical nature
framed them for you,
to spin under, fall under.
Just for you.
I hope we're born again
as highways, as prayer cards, as beer, as memory,
as all the things that connect me to you,
just you.

The only place
where waters flow East and West
and a continent is divided: Home.

Fall is coming.
Do you know who lost 11 yearlings?
Do you know who broke the rake?
Do you know who is sleeping alone?
Blowing quickly down the plains,
no wind break, no deadfall,
nothing but the cold gossip.
Fall is coming.

And you run to the door
to turn a key,

remembrance clouds reality.

Tears, as you exit and drive,
down and around
a totaled mess of a car,

rolled on the side of the Interstate,
frozen, in time.

And, we can't not look.

An insurmountable desire for change,
indirection, scars the landscape
of dry riverbeds and small streams,
fed by springs of water that never freeze,
sanguinary and alive.

The smallest drops of rain,
from a sudden, emotional, torrential, cloudburst
absorb with immediacy
into the red clay,
cracked by Summer.

Your wet shoes carry you forward,
perplexed, shocked,
unwilling to remember,
so you just turn the key.

Do you remember the snow in June?
Do you remember her with those Prime Times?
Do you remember anything?
Blowing through the brown grass,
no wind break, no deadfall,
nothing but the cold gossip.
Fall is coming.

A natural decision,
drive for purpose,
unfolds as the instant ditch
created by a flash flood
of sentimentality,
a choice of East or West
and freedom.

Or is that the past?

Do you know?

Do you remember?

Fall is coming.

Reality of choice
implies the ferocious
weather of life,
in season
and out,
in the least populated state.

And still I wonder,
after short Summertime,
after the Fall,
does Spring always follow Winter?

They say, it was a conspiracy when they poisoned her,
the only woman convicted of cattle rustling.
We have her place now,
a few run down houses on fields,
dried since the mine diverted the water,
and yet we still bale hay here, doggedly.
There's never much.

Haying

It's all about patterns, geometry,
spilled diesel around the pump.

Beautiful, tragic, money.

"But the hay's good this year."

Spit.

It's about screwing up, missing corners,
being too late,

"I lost the pattern."

Spit.

It's about the talk:
"The hay's good this year."
It's about patterns,
making it year to year,
cyclical.

Spit.

Wyoming is one big small town
with really long roads,
geometric,
an easy roadmap.

And, even on the Interstate
you know who's driving by,
or at least where they're from.

The counties are numbered,
and that number's on each license plate,
and County 3 is Sheridan,
and County 12 is Lincoln,

and County 2 is the capitol,
and County 5 is Albany,
and so on, and so on,
and there are only a few big towns
in each county.

I still talk poetry to people who don't get it,
(or do they),
but that's haying
(or is it).

I fear staying out there too long,
though they poisoned her over a hundred years ago,
but, like they say, it was a conspiracy,
and, like they say, it was a friend of her's,
and so I wonder,
"Who in the hell was that man on the gray horse?"

Camelot Has Fallen

1.
I wish Yellowstone would erupt,
covering the hills
made by the inland sea
in soot,
leaving a hole
of empty emotion,
establishing a purgatorial
cleansing flame
to turn dark sage
and black clay
into white ash.

2.
I naturally forgot,
and left you behind,
a memory of childhood
or a dream.

You are fleeting,
a figment of 'magination,
a creation almost of Hollywood
and an age gone by,
where cars were fast
and life was faster,
so naturally I forgot.

You smoked
and drank,
something we have in common.
The George Jones,
played too loud,
is just the same,
now as in 1969.

I wonder if you thought in terms of death.

At seventy years young,
she is younger still
than my seventy year old soul.

But what of age
that comes to an end?
When I'm alone?
I wonder if she thought in terms of death.

The next question
to ask (to answer), to be forgot:
what do you think of her old boyfriends?
Asked over black and white faces,
slicked hair, thick glasses.
We lock eyes.
Most of them are dead
or naturally forgot.

I wonder if he thinks in terms of death because this is the third time he
    asked, and, of course, he naturally forgot.

3.
Sunflowers were always her favorite.
She'd sing,
you are my sunshine.

They are flowers
for weddings and births,
bright, bringing joy.

My only sunshine,
they grow in ditches
along the roads,
in front of dilapidated houses,
broken homes,
bringing joy,
you'd think.

She hid the stolen beef in the walls,
insulated from the heat;
she was supposed to be pretty,
but a man's woman.
Maybe that's why they were okay putting her away,
apparently someone didn't think it was enough,
the man on the gray horse.
But we all die younger here,
and that's the conspiracy.

And so I wonder, who stays here,
and, why?

Isolation

1.
We have all been the Moor.
We have all been the traitor.
We have all been the outsider.

We have all been the body looking through the windows
but separated.

2.
Exclusion is no great deal,
but intensity, profound.

We are the new protagonist,
the hero aware of his weakness, autobiography,
three movements in the creation of a seminal work:
morning, midday, dusk.

As the birds fly,
unified breathing begets motion,
begets change, as the birds fly.

3.
Amid briar,
and flame.

And the scar,
deep and layered,
but temporary.

Exclusion,
kinetic mass, blown by wind,
as ash, rattling the windows,
looking within,
where we don't belong.

4.
Amid the ashes, grow roses,

grow sunflowers,
or something near.

The next question to ask (to answer), to be forgot:
do you take the Interstate?

The pattern, cyclical,
there and back,
there and back,
seems off today.

Do you remember,
the smell of vanilla,
the flowers, wild, sunflowers,
the gossip,
the highways,
the memory?

The only place
where waters flow East and West
and a continent is divided: Home.

You drive,
there or back,
for purpose, any purpose,
but you'll forget
as remembrance clouds reality.

Indirection frames this drive,
called to attention by the dead,
saints and sinners,
shit,
this is getting sentimental.

Do you remember?
Do you know?
Do you get it?

Isolation.

But that's life in the least populated state,

so it's really no great deal,
and, naturally, you'll forget
no matter how many times you ask.

Let the Dead Bury the Dead

If you ask, they'll tell you
how to stick a dollar bill to the ceiling.
And, naturally, you'll forget.

The regulars have changed: they're young.
The banter hasn't.
He said, she said.
That "Shoulda coulda woulda" and
the "Here's to you and here's to me."

So I wonder:
Would Hemingway like it here?
Would he like the bar's name?
Freedom's Edge.

Naturally, one might ask:
Who does like it here?

That question remains,
everyone wonders about it.
Even the Press;
they just released an article
saying my hometown is the most underrated town in America.

The Mint Bar;
it makes the list of sites in town.
I've been,
everybody's been.
As the billboard says,
"Meet me at the Mint."

Or meet Hemingway at the Mint.
He drank down the street once
before he went up the mountain;
they've got his desk,
Hemingway's Desk,
where he finished a book and a story,
in a cabin
in the woods.

Up Red Grade Road,
sans pavement.
How the hell did he do it?

Pragmatic.
You'll know what to expect.

The walls of the Mint are covered in Ranch brands:
wood panels burned with
the same irons
as the animals.

Decorative.

My family's brand isn't displayed,
and if people ask,
it's because we run sheep,

and ours is displayed on the other side of the state,
where you can drink for free
because the owner's a cousin,
the Stock Exchange Club.

The Mint's brands are older still,
like the Englishmen who set up camp
and the most underrated town around.
All the tourists ask the locals if they have a brand displayed
and if the bartender doesn't really know anything,
he'll tell you to look for a picture
on the wall
of a horse drinking at the bar.

Hemingway liked it here.

There is a fear,
in the isolation of a state,
where all know all, but hardly see one another,
that you will be forgotten,
a shit legacy.

Maybe that's why
I don't like death;
I ignore it when I can.
Like the conversation tonight.

We see more than we understand,
but they especially don't understand.

The loss of memory,
that childish talk that is used to address the old men
because we don't know how to talk to them anymore,
naturally, that changes how you think of legacy.
I imagine that's why we all die younger here,
and I imagine that's why so many old men sit at the bar every day,
running from something or to something,
but I'm getting too poetic here
and I'll eventually sound romantic.
Still that very real inability to grasp at choice makes me, naturally, appeal
    to the sentimental.

There's no good fishing in this part of the state,
that's how I know Hemingway wouldn't like it here,
but he might admire that no nonsense approach to the hungover morning,
brew the coffee,
drink the coffee,
head out.

But a drive
across the state
brings you back to the mountain,
his mountain,
where they have his desk.

I drove up to it,
I did better than he did,
I imagine.
They must have fixed the road.
It looked good.
But, shit, I still wonder,
how the hell did he do it?
It seems so long ago and it was,
a time of romance and violence
and strength,
and so he did it.

Crazy.

I get it.
I drove up there,
resigned,
sat at his desk,
and wrote.

Hemingway's Desk

Running from crazy in a circular room,
dusty footprints going round and round;
he can't trap you in a corner,
going round and round until you tire.
Or he tires. Or you both tire.
A dizzying drunken standstill,
eyeing each other across the diameter,
colliding as you stop (he stops).

Resigned. Running from crazy
or to crazy.
Dusty footprints converge,
embracing as they go,
going crazy.
Converging on the desk,
we've quit running,
together: resigned.

Rings of whiskey, scratches of pen,
knives and blood, bleeding on paper;
the continual round and round
of dusty footprints,
running from crazy.
Resigned. Writing.

I get it, at least I think I do.
But, shit, I still wonder,
who is crazier, him or me?

How did he really die?
A morning after a few too many beers.
The need for a purpose.
Legacy.
It was a conspiracy, I'm sure.
You ask; they'll tell you,
but who goes crazy here, and why?
Who does die here, and why?

Prayer Cards

When death appears outside
of conceptual grasp,
I call horse shit,
Muero porque no muero.
That changes things,
among the horse shit,
on boots and floorboards,
when you're running late,
Santa Teresa of Ávila
calls you to attention,
passing attention,
reminding you death's no thing.

I saw five elk today,
over coffee, in the car.

The wilderness gone,
I remembered the 47 bulls
up Watercress,
that spot of the old house,
purple and blue and white in winter's light,
frozen and hard.
They hopped the fence.

These did not, at least today.

Surrounded by inundations of paper,
sacred and wounded hearts,
Precious Bloods of Sorrowful Passions,
no greater love:
the Good Shepherd,
a bleeding shepherd,
among the sheep
papal and pastoral,
you see him
on the dash,
staring back with glossy eyes on glossy paper.

A secret yearning,
a homesickness for a past
ephemeral and gone,
exists in us,
who exist, only in imagination.

It's like the rain,
the smell of it, afterwards,
a common memory,
lost until the next storm.

For God's sake,
why? You ask.
To be reminded,
tomorrow may never enter your soul.
Saint Faustina
offers a relic of mercy
on longer drives
for other drives.

In memory of,
reads another,
a man I never knew,
Father Cornelius O'Connor,
(May he rest in peace.)
a subtle reminder
to remember
that person that day
but not every day.

Life giving, sustaining, washing
is the rain
that doesn't exist out here,
where we exist only in memory.

At least that's what they think.
Reality is tricky,

where our misery is our own, alone.

I once knew a priest
who hit an elk,
in the winter,
with a friend in the passenger seat.

The priest broke his neck,
so did the elk.

And today,
I find myself alone,
on another drive,
a longer drive.
No-name towns quickly pass by, filled by a handful of people
I will never know,
especially if tomorrow never comes.
At this speed, how could I rest in peace?

We see more than we understand,
especially in the harsh light of morning,
striking in comparison to the soft illumination of dusk,
that reminds you, "Today was an alright day."

That slow walk to the kitchen coffee,
that hungover feel even if you weren't really drinking the night before,
adds character to the budding day of quiet work,
alone,
out there,
along the fencelines and among the brush,
pungent in the dew.

Springtime

The electric hum of a beating heart is Springtime,
an eerie hum, unnatural,
that hum under the powerlines
that makes a horse uncomfortable
and kills your radio.

Those powerlines run to California,
the West,
that place where we don't exist,
and it makes you feel alone,
the hum.

The songbirds fly low to the ground,
frightened or adapted,
as we ride,
the air charged,
through the sagebrush.

Your hair stands up,
like the wildflowers,
static and kinetic,
pulling you up or West,
and you just want to get out.

Lambs upset tender nests
to gallop and leap ahead,
crying, as we sort,
Springtime.

Electric air churns overhead,
pulsing, diastolic,
as the powerlines wave
like the new leaves
on the brush,
whispering of something to come,
or nothing.

Flow and space,
like art,
like the Interstate,
like hay falling,
like beer from the tap filling a stein,
at Freedom's Edge, drawn out and away.
You know, this place has changed,
I never saw the original
Freedom's Edge,
too young,
but I listened to a cover band
explain a song they wrote about
Freedom's Edge,
literal or figurative,
I don't know for sure,
like if it actually existed.

People talk like it did,
again, that's a legacy.
And, I'm not being completely fair;
Freedom's Edge is really a brewery,
but, of course and naturally, I wish it was a dive bar.
Somehow that seems more fitting.

We see more than we understand,
like how the grass looks greener
in the dusk,
and how at the same time,
the talk dies
so that we can absorb whatever's left
before the light fades,
giving way to the neon stops along the highway.
It'll pick up again,
the talk.

I mentioned this once
to some guy on his way through to Sturgis;
actually, I'm pretty sure he was some long lost cousin of mine.
He looked at me with the built in bullshit detector
we all have out here,
but what I said
wasn't bullshit,
and he knew it,
that's why the talk, naturally, went nowhere.

Fences need fixed to keep strays out,
to carve out fierce individualism
in a spot where it is all too easy to be swallowed up.

There is a solidarity in the isolation of the state,
and you either get it or you don't.
Don't get left behind,
it's cyclical, time,
and it doesn't wait for us.

Again, that's legacy.
I wonder if that's what Mother Nature does with dusk,
offering one last shot,
when the grass is greener,
to make you say,
"Today was an alright day."

Stained Glass of St. Meinrad's

Skulls
and Vespers,
memorialized in whispers
on the glass,
remind me of Winter.

The empty,
frozen Church
of those snowy months
is Compline,
yet unrealized, but expected,
when the innermost
chamber of the soul
is like an icebox.

But, in prophesy, hope,
a boat
stranded
in a frozen lake,
becomes a reservoir
of light,
asleep,
resting in His peace.

Still, now,
before the snows,
the skulls
and Vespers
return an Autumn warning
of the cold
ground of Compline,
hard, like hearts,
O, ye of little faith.

Does Spring always follow Winter?
When there is no thaw,
let the dead bury the dead.

He died.
And, they talked about it at the bar.
I couldn't do that,
but my face could show
a look of remorse
or sadness.

That's not a bad legacy,
as most people would talk.

It is good.
It is very good.
But I fear it,
the talk that is,
and just drink my beer.

I Am Happy Here

The talk began once the fire started.
I said.
He said.
I said.
He said.
In the waning light of day,
the talk turned away from less serious things.

"Did you see your old, red truck?"

"Yeah, I'm surprised the piece of shit still runs."
I laugh.
"Remember when it burned through all its coolant, and I was stuck on the side of the highway for over an hour, waiting on your ass?"

"Hey now, I got you home! But we had bottles of coolant stacked in the back like plywood."

We drank the whiskey, slowly, straight, in the firelight.
This was different talk.

We see more than we know,
like the signs along the highway.
I feel like most of the world ignores signposts
because they're more preoccupied
with other cars and pedestrians.

Instead, we notice them all
because we can drive for hours on Interstate
and see no more than a handful of people.

I wonder how the roads got their names,
Crazy Woman,
Tunnel,
Remount,
Harriman Road, that sounds like a name,
like the old place, the one we renamed,
Angelo's.

Maybe somebody knew once,
how the names came to be,
the old men before the memory failed.
But that's all hearsay, a conspiracy,
just like that man on the gray horse.

"Why don't you come back here? I miss you and want you to be a part of this. The Dream Team. I'll be Bobby and you be Jack."

"You are my Bobby!"

We laugh.

"I think the future is up for grabs, if you come back, a part of it will be yours. I can run things and you do the politicking. We'd work side by side with the sheep and the men. We'd have fun, and, maybe, I'd love it again."

Sentimentality seems so misplaced.
The immediacy of life and choice out here,
the in-your-face reality that we all die younger,
unravels a wave of ferocious energy I can't place except for coming from
    the soil.

And, still, we stay,
and, still, I wonder who does leave this place and why?

I think, "He just doesn't get it."
But that's typical.

"Come on, cousin, I need you here."

"I know." I get it. I say it pragmatically.

I let it die, the talk.

It's like choosing an exit;
knowing which road to take with our eyes closed,
we've done it so many times
driving across our little state,
never out,
but we still read the signs,
every time,
just to make sure we chose right.

"He's fading fast."

"I know. That's why I'm here. You know, listen to how your brother talks to him; it's like he doesn't know how to anymore. It's like he's talking to a baby. He's not dead yet."

"Don't you wish it could be over."

"No."

He'll still tell you the old stories,
about how it was all a conspiracy.
And, we'll talk about it around the fire,
shivering.

I stand, sway a little,
and walk to the tall grass, black in the night,
and piss.

"Look at the stars. You can't see them that close to the fire."

"I'll wait till you're done. I have to piss too."

I walk back and refill my cup.

"There's nowhere else I'd rather be, cousin."

"Then stay."

"I can't."

"You would be happy here."

"I am happy here."

"Shut up," and I fill his cup.

There's no certainty out here, but I imagine there's no certainty anywhere. I wouldn't know, I haven't been anywhere.

Still that very real inability to grasp at choice makes me, naturally, appeal to the sentimental.

Again, I don't know why. Maybe it's in the soil.

We can hear frogs in the irrigation ditches and the crackle of the fire.
I lean back and pull out some cheap cigars.
We smoke, thinking.

"Why do you want to stay here? You were saying last week you wished
you woulda taken that job in Provo."

"Hell, I'd only want to do that for a while. I'd want to be back."

"Yeah. You'd make more money there."

"I know."

We smoke in silence, listening to the frogs and the fire;
the smoke joins that rising from the logs.

To Be Read Almost In Real Time

The darkness of solitude,
envelops the cold
that presses in and nips at ears,
noses that smell the warmth of firelight
and ever burning pine logs
that measure time
in fleeting minutes of heat.

The stars align above frostbit ears
and a record snow,
measuring time in inches
and feet and footprints
left by solitary pilgrims
who seek catharsis
and Truth
by the fire.

I sometimes feel so alone out here,
but that's okay,
just don't get swallowed up, you know.
It's hard to imagine leaving.

The next question
to ask (to answer), to be forgot:
(?)

That very real inability to grasp at choice,
or chance,
or risk.
I keep coming back to that.
I want *you* to understand,
where the others don't get it.
But there's no judgement there
if you don't get it.
I just want you to get it;
it's just that idea that
you're going somewhere,
and the others aren't going somewhere.

Risk, to risk to be lost,

to (not) be forgotten,

to (not) leave County 12,

to (not) be isolated,

to (not) follow the pattern, cyclical (or not),

to (not) leave the bar or (not) meet me at the Mint,

to (not) live for the talk,

to (not) get sentimental,

to (not) laugh and (not) drink around a fire,

to (not) wish it could all be over,

to (not) risk differently,

to (not) die younger here.

It's about choice,
that's it; it's said pragmatically,

do we (not) live for this (not) legacy,

do you (not) live for this (not) legacy,

because we all die younger here.

I was never really sure if you were going to understand me,
to get this.
It's okay, but try.
I need you,
I need you to try.

So, for going somewhere,
I risk being lost,
or losing,
someone or something,
because for everything I gain,
something is lost,
and I don't want it to be you.

Kaycee, Wyoming
Population: 263

You can see my grandfather's house from the Interstate,
I know that,
but I never know which one it is,
the little house or the double-wide.
I usually assume it's the double-wide.

I passed his house today,
driving home;
it looked snowed-in.
The drifts creeping in on all sides,
like impending death,
a heart attack or stroke
that could, couldn't, be prevented.
But, we all die younger here.

I had met him once,
as a baby, I don't remember.
I assume it was awkward,
not for me, but her,
his daughter, my mother,
as they chatted
about things held in common:
the weather,
his new grandchild.

But there was no embrace,
no warmth,
just awkward guilt,
justified by nonexistent faith
and works of mercy and violence.

Soon after, he came into the hospital,
near Riverton,
when she worked the night shift.
drunk, he stumbled
into the highway, going home,

and was hit, by a speeding car.
He died.
The whiskey bottle
unbroken in his pocket
as she cut the clothes
from his broken body.
It could, couldn't, be prevented,
but, we all die younger here.

That question still remains,
and the Press just released another article,
about Wyoming
scoring lowest on some sort of childhood wellbeing scale.
I believe it.
It's that same idea.
We don't wear seat belts when we drive,
we risk differently.
We still smoke and drink,
we think differently.
There's a surety in that immediacy,
that buzz.
Instant gratification,
we know what's coming,
and that makes it easy.
For example, you can't do much in winter,
but, that's easy.
We're equipped for that.
We know what'll happen,
and we still might try to move the soil,
but, naturally, the ground is too hard to dig,
and we can talk,
and say, I knew better,
and shit,
and better wait for the thaw,
and wanna get a drink?
No risk there.
In fact, the only thing that implies uncertainty
is leaving,
or being left.
But that's a different story,
when you're going somewhere and
everyone else isn't going somewhere.

But that's a ways away,
and the weatherman,
the winds,
is always wrong.

The winds that come from the West,
the Chinook,
from that manifestation of Freedom,
the coast,
to announce short lived Spring.

In the warm months,
when the rain mars the placid water
of a high altitude lake
and the fish sink into the depths,
the psychiatric treatment of the drops
breaks the shock of a bright, warm day
and summer's random heat.

Freezing rain,
cold in the heat,
turns to snow
in a heartbeat,
a heartache,
and we, westerners,
know winter is around
the next bend in the highway,
bringing ice and accidents.
So, it's better to stay at home.
But, healthy cynicism,
quotes Henry,
makes us American,
and western,
as the winds,
the weatherman who tries.

All we have is Mother Nature,
we can't beat her,
and winter is our favorite season.

That very real inability to grasp at chance makes me, naturally, appeal to the sentimental.

We're pushed out
and pulled back,
that ferocious energy,
from the soil,
our cruel soil.

A slip of the pen.

From the soul,
our cruel soul,

because we have all we need out here,
between the Mint
and the Stock Exchange,
and Freedom's Edge.

Shit, that's a good name.

Because our soul,
the soil,
is Freedom's Edge,
and it lends itself to moving on,
even just for a while,
but that's easy to say,
hard to hear.

And that is what we mean when we say,
I know,
and, I'd want to be back,
and, there's no certainty out here.
But, there is a certainty,
a legacy;
you can't fail
because of the talk.
Otherwise, there is no certainty out here.
That's it, it's said pragmatically,
and, thus, who would want to leave and why?

To risk differently,
I mean,
there's inherent risk,
like when the roads turn to ice
or a ground blizzard creeps across the Interstate,
but that's just a part of life out here,
and that's something we get,
like that cruel soil,
the soil that, they say,
"Ain't worth shit,"
unless it's worked,
which might be true,
but then why do it at all.
It's a paradox of the land,
less people, more impact,
and I just can't get into that sentimentality right now,
and that's what people don't get.
We risk differently
out here,
because that ice, that blizzard,
doesn't scare us.
The only risk is if that storm doesn't come,
that's what I need you to understand.

One might ask, naturally:
Who does leave this place and why?

Survival

1.
Being Young Once

The Wind:
>Where are you going, old friend?
>A poem is not just living,
>but living again.
>The past remains vivid,
>but I am losing it,
>or never had it all together.

Together:
>We remember back,
>the way back,
>to let go of what we think
>we know.
>Will you be left behind?

The Wild:
>Set yourself free
>in the search for freedom.
>Sometimes the moment is enough.
>There are more important things,
>the wind for one.

2.
Buford, Wyoming
Population: 1

Into the wild,
the words roll over the hills
and hit snow fence,
gas station (overpriced),
and Interstate.

Undeterred, they continue.
"SOS" this is no joke.
The road has always led West.

Still, I drive East,
hyperkinetic,
wishing to choose West
with finality.

3.
Wanderers of the Wasteland

Nemo was lost in Mormon Country.
Villa disappeared out on the desert.
And, Alejandro, one of the hired men, a sheepherder, rolled an ATV.

We still ride, only ride,
finding lonely places,

hiding nothing.
Or everything.

The shepherd lives a solitary life,
monastic and pensive,
speaking in tongues
only animals understand.

But what do we run from?
The need for a purpose.

4.
Time moves slower here;
it's god awful cold,
29 below,
and everything's fighting for survival.
I counted the seconds
between a first and second kiss,
between a trigger pulled and a dead bunny.
Blood stains the snow,
as the wind pushes the cold,
lower and deeper,

29 below.
I watched the crow fly,
circling above as I counted.
One, two, three.
I watched her walk away,
then drove into the storm.
Standing still in time,
the trailer swayed in the wind
and fell, dragging it all down.
I counted the seconds,
and time moves slower here.

There's something cyclical about the soil:
Plant, irrigate, reap, wait, plant, irrigate, reap, wait.
There's something cyclical about life,
out here.
There's a risk that you'll get swallowed up.
Actually, that one's a given,
that's why it's so easy to stay here.
At least you know what's coming,
and that's a different sentimentality.

Wyoming Songs

1.
It's fitting,
if you're on a horse
in winter, near twilight,
facing a storm,
to think of the Wyoming songs.
I've done it before.

The frost gathers
on the horse's eyelashes
and the cold
grips your numb fingers,
making them useless
on the reins,
luckily, the horse knows the way.

Steaming, the two of you
work towards home,
the only sound,
the squeak of snow
under hoof,
breaking trail
among the humps
of snow covered sagebrush.

And still I wonder,
does Spring always follow Winter?

I feel as if I'm going to lose you, here,
but maybe that's okay.
But, then again, I feel as if I'm going to *lose* you,
and I can't feel that way.

I feel this loss, like that damn letter,
that damn poem
that everyone still talks about,
even though no one remembers the words.
I've tried to imagine it,
but that's all it is a memory, maybe imagined,
and it's still lost.

I can't lose you.
That's a scary thought,
like if I came back,
drove into town,
passed Freedom's Edge,
passed the Mint,
passed the Stock Exchange,
and what if we didn't stop to talk?
Or did,
and had nothing to say?
But maybe that's okay,
I'll still try to remember,
but it'll naturally be forgot,
and that letter will still be out here,
somewhere.

Wyoming Songs

2.
There once was a song,
a poem of the plains,
a Sheepherder's Song,
lost as old-timers died off.
Written in camp
and mailed home for Christmas,
it read of snow and sheep,
of poverty and cold
near the brush-fueled fire,
melting water for the horses.

It sighed and shook with life,
even as the cold
suffocated and killed,
as sheep died along the river,
their noses frozen to the ground.

The lines rose
in joyous antiphons,
noting the arrival of lambs and pups
and Springtime.
They sunk as wolves circled round,
round and round,
seeking tender flesh.
They steadied,
mirroring an ever-beating heart
that brought necessary continuity.

It grew from page to page,
to be read almost in real time
as you think of the herder there,
in the snow,
surviving another night
on mutton and sheepskin blankets,
with collies over feet
and under head.

Legends never die,
the talk never dies.
Because it is all about legacy in the end.
Like that man on that damned gray horse,
or her.
My life isn't so different from theirs
because out here it's still 1886.
It's cyclical, that ferocious energy that swallows us up
and holds us in, like roots in that damn cruel, hard, unforgiving soil,
the make or break, that in-your-face reality.
It's as if memory, the talk,
exists on its own,
in real time,
parallel to the now,
that eternal now
of immediate gratification.
Parallel until memory swerves suddenly
to intersect our reality,
swallowing us up into that moment,
and if I stay, I will die younger here.

Do I wish it could be over?
No.

They say, it was a conspiracy.

It is good.
It is very good.
Of choice,
or chance,
or risk.

Maybe that's okay.

In a spot where it is all too easy to be swallowed up.

But I fear it,
the talk that is,
and just drink my beer.

Tyler Truman Julian spent his life moving around the state of Wyoming, until his parents settled in Sheridan, just south of the Montana border. Once there, he split time between Sheridan and Kemmerer, the site of the family sheep ranch in southwestern Wyoming. He attended the University of Wyoming and received degrees in International Studies and Spanish Literature. Eventually and with some prodding, he remembered the call he felt as a child to become a writer. He currently attends New Mexico State University, where he is a graduate student in their MFA Program, studying fiction. He lives in Mesilla, NM, with his wife. He has several projects in the works and is actively sending out submissions to journals. His work has appeared in *Oasis, Burnt Pine Magazine, Wyoming Magazine,* and *Cigar City Poetry Journal. For more information, visit www.tylertrumanjulian.com.*

CPSIA information can be obtained
at www.ICGtesting.com
Printed in the USA
FFHW020957250319
51221232-56701FF